The Battle of Wake Island: The History of the Japanese Invasion Launched in Conjunction with the Attack on Pearl Harbor

By Charles River Editors

A picture of Japanese patrol boats around Wake Island

About Charles River Editors

Charles River Editors is a boutique digital publishing company, specializing in bringing history back to life with educational and engaging books on a wide range of topics. Keep up to date with our new and free offerings with this 5 second sign up on our weekly mailing list, and visit Our Kindle Author Page to see other recently published Kindle titles.

We make these books for you and always want to know our readers' opinions, so we encourage you to leave reviews and look forward to publishing new and exciting titles each week.

Introduction

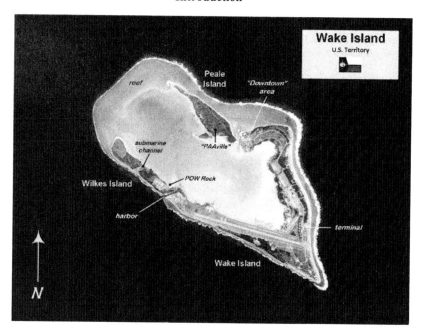

A map of Wake Island

The Battle of Wake Island (December 1941)

All Americans are familiar with the "day that will live in infamy." At 9:30 a.m. on Sunday, December 7, 1941, Pearl Harbor, the advanced base of the United States Navy's Pacific Fleet, was ablaze. It had been smashed by aircraft launched by the carriers of the Imperial Japanese Navy. All eight battleships had been sunk or badly damaged, 350 aircraft had been knocked out, and over 2,000 Americans lay dead. Indelible images of the USS *Arizona* exploding and the USS *Oklahoma* capsizing and floating upside down have been ingrained in the American conscience ever since. In less than an hour and a half the Japanese had almost wiped out America's entire naval presence in the Pacific, but one of the aspects of the war most forgotten is that the Japanese simultaneously launched concerted attacks against American targets elsewhere in the Pacific that the same day, including one against the strategically located Wake Island.

Isolated in the dark blue vastness of the west-central Pacific Ocean, the tiny chevron-shaped island of Wake, surrounded by barrier reefs, possessed outsized strategic significance during

World War II. Originally discovered by the Spanish navigator Álvaro de Mendaña y Neira in 1568 as he explored the Pacific in his ships *Los Reyes* and *Todos Santos*, the island's inhospitable aspect kept the daring Spaniard from landing or even naming his discovery. It fell to another explorer, this one English – Samuel Wake, captain of the Prince William Henry – to name the island in 1796, though he also declined to land.

These men refused to attempt reaching the shore due to the violent currents and gigantic surf around Wake, caused by the fact that the edges of Wake drop off 12,000 feet into the deep ocean. No continental shelf mitigates the strength or violence of the open ocean waters, and Wake Island also lacks any source of fresh water other than rain. Typhoons periodically swamp the atoll, whose highest point stands 21 feet above sea level.

Claimed for the United States in 1841 by the cheerful, narrow-faced Lieutenant Charles Wilkes aboard the USS Vincennes, Wake Island (actually three separate portions known as Wake, Peale, and Wilkes Islands) remained essentially useless until the technology and politics of the 20th century suddenly rendered it more important. Given the possibility of war with Japan in the near future, the United States Navy began researching and developing the island for use as a forward airbase in 1940. Located between Hawaii and Japan, with the nearest inhabited land over 600 miles away, Wake appeared as a key strategic asset for America. Its status as U.S. territory made it possible for the Navy to construct a base there without antagonizing the Japanese, and desalination technology enabled maintaining a permanent human presence on the island. Admiral Husband E. Kimmel, CINCPAC in 1941, prepared a long commentary on Wake which included the assessment: "The strategic importance of Wake is increasingly evident, as one inquires into means by which the Pacific Fleet may carry on offensive operations to the westward. […] As an operating patrol plane base, it could prove highly valuable to us in observing the Marshalls, or in covering advance of our forces toward the Saipan-Honshu line. In the hands of the Japanese, it would be a serious obstacle to surprise raids." (Heinl, 1947, 1).

The Japanese, of course, also recognized the strategic value of Wake and planned to deny it to the United States. Since their war plan involved a surprise attack, with the declaration of war following the start of hostilities, they anticipated seizing Wake Island with minimal resistance from the contractors and U.S. Marines there. The Japanese might perhaps have viewed the Americans on Wake in the same way Shakespeare's Duke of Orleans dismissed the English in Henry V, Act III, Scene 7: "You may as well say, that's a valiant flea that dare eat his breakfast on the lip of a lion." As it turned out, the Japanese would require multiple invasion attempts and a few weeks to take the island against dogged American resistance, and it would cost them over 1,000 casualties by the time the fighting was finished.

The Battle of Wake Island: The History of the Japanese Invasion Launched in Conjunction with the Attack on Pearl Harbor chronicles one of the initial Japanese campaigns in the Pacific. Along with pictures of important people, places, and events, you will learn about the battle like never before.

The Battle of Wake Island: The History of the Japanese Invasion Launched in Conjunction with the Attack on Pearl Harbor

Chapter 1: Before the Battle

Given the way the war turned out, some historians have asserted that World War II actually started years before Germany's invasion of Poland but with Japan's invasion of China. Japan had been fighting a costly and expansive war in China since 1937 and had invaded Manchuria six years earlier. Though Euro-centric observers at the time (and hordes of later historians) focused on the drama of the European powers, the fighting in Asia represented war on a previously unknown scale. In the notorious "Rape of Nanking", 200,000 Chinese civilians were killed. Asia thus had its own hegemonic dictatorship marching across the map, as the people of Indo-China discovered in September 1940. Korea had been under the Japanese yoke since 1910. Indeed, Japan was now openly allied with Hitler and Mussolini under the terms of the "Pact of Steel", signed in 1939.

As with Europe, the United States initially played a cautious game vis-à-vis their stance toward Japan. After all, America was a democratic continental power secure in her own borders and with a strong tradition of isolationism. This attitude was strengthened by her historic hostility towards empire. Why should American lives be shed in a conflict which seemed to be yet another example of the old empires fighting it out for real estate?

Once the Germans invaded the Soviet Union, the Japanese no longer needed to worry about their border with Russia, allowing them to focus exclusively on expanding across the Far East and various islands in the Pacific. But by then the Japanese leadership faced a difficult strategic dilemma. Their ambition to build a large Asian empire could not be realized without the defeat of China, and the Chinese war had descended into a quagmire. A Japanese victory in China remained just about plausible, but in order to secure one Japan needed to maintain a large army on the continent almost indefinitely. In short, the war was draining vast quantities of resources and had become attritional.

Given their undoubted qualitative superiority over Chinese forces, the Japanese probably had the manpower, the technology and the tactics to eventually beat the divided Chinese opposition. Their bigger problem was a lack of natural resources, particularly oil and rubber. For these vital resources, Japan relied heavily on imports from European colonies like British Malaya, and it relied on the United States for most of its oil. Now, however, Japan found itself in a vicious circle of its own making; Japan's aggressive foreign policy in Asia and its alliance with the Axis had alienated these sources. In response to Japanese aggression in China and other places, the United States had imposed a crippling embargo suspending crucial oil exports to Japan in early 1941. Japan's war effort was being severely undermined because the suppliers of its resources were so opposed to it.

Therefore, although Japan's main ambition was an empire centered on China and continental eastern Asia, this resource squeeze forced it to look southward. The Japanese came up with the notion of a "Southern Resource Area", a plan by which Japan would seize control of British

Malaya and the Dutch East Indies in order to fuel the conquest and economic exploitation of the main empire in China. In other words, Japan did not look to or wish for a war with the United States per se; it planned to target the colonies held by old European imperial powers that had quite enough on their plates in Europe.

Perhaps fatefully, Japan was of the opinion that an attack on British targets in the Pacific would inevitably bring war with America. From a modern perspective this appears a questionable analysis, given America's strong isolationist sentiments. For Japan in 1941 though, there was a chain of logic which ran from a need to secure resources to the identification of targets in the Pacific to the need to confront America.

At the same time, Roosevelt faced a dilemma too. Though he had won a fairly easy election in 1940, the key issue during the presidential election of 1940 had been the expanding war. Both mainstream candidates adopted an isolationist stance, with FDR promising that American boys "are not going to be sent to any foreign war". It was clear that majority opinion across the nation took the understandable view that the country could and should stay out of World War II. Roosevelt however, had a more nuanced personal opinion. He saw that it was not tenable for the United States to operate in a world system dominated by dictatorships. Sooner or later, these irrational and violent regimes would threaten America as well. That was a hard-nosed strategic and political insight.

Furthermore, there was a moral position to be taken here: arguably, it was simply not right for a power of America's weight to stand by while freedom was snuffed out in the most brutal manner across much of the planet. The Nanking massacre, the bombing of Rotterdam, and the persecution of the Jews were all issues that mattered to moral men, and Roosevelt's personal views were if anything strengthened by his relationship with Winston Churchill, Britain's bulldog prime minister. Churchill was completely uncompromising in his attitude toward the Axis, and equally firm in his opinion that the free world needed American help. While Roosevelt's attitude to Churchill and the British would cool in later years, by 1941 he had developed a deep respect for their brave stand against Nazi Germany and fascist Italy.

Roosevelt was also a skilled democratic politician. In this he practiced politics as "the art of the possible", which was as much about leading and persuading the people as it was about simply acting as their delegate. Roosevelt had become increasingly convinced that the nation would eventually be drawn into World War II; his dilemma was securing public support for the action that he deemed to be necessary. This position, evidenced by the Administration's close support for Britain's war effort, fed the suspicions of the isolationists at the time and has contributed to a more modern debate about the Pearl Harbor attack. Did Roosevelt, as some revisionist historians have maintained, deliberately provoke Japan's attack or even withhold intelligence from his military in order to increase the shock when it occurred? The debate about the "Back Door to War" theory continues to linger, even as it attracts less support than it once did. It is clear that

Roosevelt believed that war would come to America sooner rather than later; but quite another thing to allege that he engineered it.

If anything, it seems far more accurate to assert that both sides misunderstood the others' position and thus unwittingly took steps that would lead to the attack on Pearl Harbor. Far from covering up evidence of an imminent Japanese attack, Roosevelt and the military planned accordingly for a Japanese attack in 1941, and one of the most obvious targets for potential Japanese expansion was the Philippines, an imperial possession still held by American forces. With a careful eye on Japan's expansion, the United States moved to protect the Philippines, which also induced President Roosevelt to station a majority of the Pacific fleet at Pearl Harbor. Japan, assuming that aggression toward British targets and the Dutch East Indies would bring the United States into the war, decided they had to inflict a blow to the United States that would set back its war effort long enough to ensure the Japanese access to enough critical resources.

Against this backdrop, the Navy hired civilian contractors to build a forward naval aviation facility and defensive works on Wake Island in July 1940. The contract went to a consortium of construction firms operating under the umbrella of CPNAB – "Contractors Pacific Naval Air Bases." However, the Morrison-Knudson company did the heavy lifting on the Wake contract, with the vigorous Harry Morrison and a cadre of veteran superintendents and foremen as the motivating spirit for the project. Nathan Teterss, a skilled 40 year old engineer, served as General Superintendent for the project. The Assistant General Superintendent, the 46 year old Harold Olson, arrived on Wake Island in January 1941 along with his oldest son, Ted Olson, then 22 years old. Olson quit a job overseeing part of the construction of the famous Grand Coulee Dam to participate in the Wake Island construction job, designated "Project 14." The number of civilian contractors working on Wake eventually reached 1,154, and since the project represented a military construction effort, Navy personnel also appeared on the island from the start. Lieutenant Commander Elmer B. Greey of the U.S. Naval Reserve functioned as the "Resident Officer-in-Charge" from the outset.

The men set about unloading a huge variety of equipment – including two heavy-duty bulldozers – and starting work immediately upon their arrival at Wake Island. Transferring materials and equipment to the island proved tricky, and the elder Olson noted the ocean conditions which daunted the early explorers enough to prevent landing: "This ocean is never calm [...] There is always a long rolling swell about ten feet high which makes the loads swing about crazily and hard to land as the barges and boats are bobbing around also. [...] Of course, this is done right in the surf and it's about as bad as riding a bucking horse." (Gilbert, 2012, 60).

The men first built a camp for themselves, which gradually acquired more amenities as time went by. Once the Marines arrived on the island and built their own camp, the civilian contractor camp acquired the name of Camp 2. The lagoon provided landing conditions for Boeing 314 Clipper flying boats. These aircraft, larger than practically any others built at the time, had a wingspan of 152 feet, a range of 3,685 miles, and carried 74 passengers along with up to 5 tons of cargo.

Operated by Pan American World Airways, the Clippers provided shuttle service to and from Honolulu, Hawaii every few days, allowing a few personnel to be moved in or out and some small, specialized equipment to be brought in. The Boeing 314s also furnished mail service, which helped to maintain morale in the challenging, harsh conditions.

The problems faced the previous year during base construction at Midway provided the men with a blueprint for more successful, faster operations on Wake. Water desalination naturally also occupied the early construction efforts of the crews, including a 50-foot water tower with a 2,000 gallon tank at its summit to supply the stills. Fresh water also proved necessary for bathing due to the irritating effect of seawater on human skin over the long term.

The workers built a steel bridge connecting the main portion of Wake Island to Peale Island, where the naval air base structures would soon rise. Other work included defensive gun positions, dredging a ship channel through the atoll into the central lagoon, and building airstrips for the expected reconnaissance plane detachments. The airstrips would soon support the Grumman F4F-3 Wildcat fighters used in the defense of Wake.

Though the men spent most of their time toiling, they still found the opportunity to examine and sometimes enjoy their surroundings. Wake Island provided a home to several species of birds, along with numerous hermit crabs. The island, in fact, housed a unique species of flightless bird, the Wake Island rail. This unfortunate species went extinct by 1945 due to the starving Japanese soldiers stationed on the atoll devouring all of the rails they could catch, wiping the birds out.

The Wake Island rail

While the well-fed Americans viewed the rails, which they called "peewees," with amusement rather than hunger, they made use of their sparse leisure time to fish. The reef, lagoon, and immediately adjacent deep water offered ample fishing of many kinds. On several occasions, the men caught sablefish weighing 75-150 pounds, along with many other, smaller varieties of fish and the occasional octopus or sea turtle.

Violent storms struck Wake during the construction, hampering efforts and damaging structures, but also providing large amounts of fresh water. The Americans had set up rain catching equipment, gaining 60,000 gallons of fresh water from a single storm whose two-hour rainfall added up to four inches. One of the men noted that the cost for desalinating an equivalent amount of sea water would amount to $10,000 ($167,748 in modern dollars).

While the work proceeded steadily and the men labored hard and with professional skill, converting the remote, rocky, storm-swept atoll into a forward airbase would end up taking more time than available before the outbreak of war in the Pacific, and the mood on Wake sobered abruptly in July when the Japanese invaded Vietnam. Peter Hansen astutely noted in an alarmed letter to his wife, "They must either get some guns and Marines here immediately or get us off the island. The Japanese owned Marshall Islands are only 300 to 500 miles south of us, it is only 1900 miles to Tokyo, and if this little island is as strategic as they claim it is they better get some guns on it right now, because if it's valuable to the U.S. it is just as valuable to Japan." (Gilbert,

2012, 128).

A detachment of US Marines indeed arrived aboard the *Regulus* in August 1941 to protect the remote American forward base. 449 Marines under Major James Devereux made up the bulk of the garrison, which totaled 524 at maximum. USN Commander Winfield Cunningham held overall authority, while Major Paul Putnam led Marine Fighting Squadron 211 with its 12 Grumman F4F-3 Wildcats.

Cunningham

Devereux

Colonel Walter Bayler of the Marine Corps left a concise, accurate picture of Wake's terrain from the perspective of a military man: "Wake is by no means the bare sandy spit one thinks of when atolls are mentioned. Considerable areas of it are covered by woods, and though the trees are small, their thick foliage and the scrubby tangled underbrush provided admirable cover. Walking in these jungles was difficult but not impossible." (Heinl, 1947, 4).

The Marines got along surprisingly well with the civilians, and their respective leaders assisted this process by keeping the men moderately segregated from one another. Meanwhile, the Marines focused on building and arming gun pits and similar emplacements, which also constituted extremely strenuous construction and hauling work. The Marines received a beer ration, unlike the civilians, but civilian food proved considerably better, leading to occasional trades. The two groups also arranged sporadic baseball games, in which the assistant superintendent's son Ted Olson distinguished himself.

Moreover, Admiral Claude Bloch, recognizing the hazardous position of Wake and the vulnerability of just 500 soldiers against the might of the Japanese empire, suggested that the Marines recruit and train civilian volunteers from among the workmen. Bloch stressed the need to not alarm the civilians unduly to prevent a mass exodus from Project 14, and recommended keeping these volunteers in "a pepped up frame of mind by jokes and their willing cooperation rather than being scared into it by fear of an outside enemy" (Gilbert, 2012,140). The Admiral's advice bore some fruit; by the time of the Japanese attack, some 300 civilian workmen fought alongside the Marines.

A picture of construction workers on Wake Island

The ominous tidings of a seemingly coming war spurred a change in construction focus towards usable facilities rather than full base infrastructure, and the Americans increased the pace of the work. Civilian workers also began quitting at a rate of 5-15 men per week, returning to Honolulu in expectation that the Japanese would attack Wake. Understandably, these men wanted to avoid being slaughtered or captured by Japanese soldiers. Nevertheless, the remaining men worked hard and completed the first runway, 5,000 feet long and 200 feet wide, by September 6th.

There was a marked asymmetry in both perceptions and capabilities as Japan and the U.S. stared each other down from across the Pacific in mid-1941. The U.S. was not ready for a Pacific war and did not want war at all, and though it was making preparations it was in no position politically or militarily to jump to the defense of the European empires in Asia. At the same time, the oil embargo indicated they were not going to underwrite Japan's aggression against China either. Without those resources, and operating under the potentially mistaken belief that aggression against Allied possessions would draw the U.S. into the war, Japan came to view the U.S. as the key obstacle to its ambitions. Both sides recognized that Japan had at least a temporary naval supremacy in 1941, and to Japan's High Command this gave them what they viewed as a small window during which to deliver a decisive blow that might secure a permanent advantage. The tectonic plates of war were shifting.

It was in this context that the idea for a crippling surprise attack against the U.S. fleet in Pearl Harbor was resurrected, planned in detail, and delivered to impressive effect. The extent to which the results of the attack were directly attributable to Japanese planning and tactical prowess is, however, more open to debate, because the idea of attacking Pearl Harbor was actually an old plan dating back nearly 15 years. Though the attack in December 1941 came as a great surprise and is still considered a daring strategy over 70 years later, such an attack had been contemplated by the Japanese High Command as early as 1927, and in 1928 Captain Isoroku Yamamoto had proposed such an attack in a lecture he gave at the Navy Torpedo School. During the 1930's, as Japan built up its navy and expanded across Asia, the concept of a strike against the U.S. Pacific Fleet gained momentum, and the Japanese had war-gamed such an attack on a number of occasions. What they had concluded was that they could expect heavy casualties, particularly if the Americans detected the Japanese fleet as it moved into position, and they were also worried about their ability to destroy battleships in harbor due to the difficulties of running torpedoes in shallow water. In overcoming that seeming disadvantage they were inadvertently aided by Britain following her successful strike against the Italian navy at Taranto, which relied exclusively on airpower.

Captain Yamamoto

The role of Yamamoto during the evolution of the plan, even as far back as the 1920's, is fundamental. A talented and charismatic leader, Yamamoto was a skilled operator able to secure the success of his own ideas within the percussive mix of Japanese military politics. Usually seen as a prescient advocate of naval airpower, Yamamoto's tactical ideas were more complex and in some ways more conservative than that. In fact, his main objective for the attack was to sink American battleships, not carriers. The idea was that the battleship, above all, reflected American military prestige and was still seen as the "Queen of the Fleet". Yamamoto believed (as did many from the dictatorships of the period) that democracies were morally weak and had a fragile will to fight. Like Hitler's assessment of the British, Yamamoto was convinced that the loss of even one battleship would be a psychological body-blow that would so demoralize American public opinion that it might secure a treaty advantageous to Japan.

Thus, when the Japanese High Command took the momentous decision to plan in earnest for a surprise attack on the American base at Pearl Harbor in 1941, it was with a view to delivering this psychological and political shock. In other words, Japan intended to deliver a message to the American people, not the American military. There was nothing new to this strategy so far as Japan was concerned; Japan's military doctrine emphasized the "will to fight" at all levels, and it had previously begun a war against Russia with a surprise assault at Port Arthur.

Unaware of the Japanese intentions but fully understanding that the pre-conflict tension mounting sharply, the U.S. sent B-17 bombers to the Philippines and Mariana Islands, among other Asian destinations. These landed on Wake for refueling once the airfield could accommodate them. With the field only partly finished, refueling represented a labor-intensive, painstaking process. Each time B-17s landed, the work slowed until they refueled and departed.

America was about to experience a very unpleasant wake-up call, due in no small part to the duplicitous nature of the Japanese government itself. On November 26, as the Japanese fleet was setting sail toward Pearl Harbor, the Roosevelt Administration gave a document to the Japanese Ambassador that consisted of two parts, one an oral statement and one an outline of a proposed basis for agreement between the United States and Japan. Of course, the Japanese High Command had already chosen war by the time the Japanese Ambassador received that document, but the ambassador himself was in the dark regarding the impending attack on Pearl Harbor. Japan's ambassador was Kurusu Saburo, and he was assisted by diplomat Nomura Kichisaburo. Together they were instructed to settle the issue by the end of November 1941, so they continued to unwittingly negotiate the terms of a peace that never had a chance, hoping against hope that they could stave off war.

As both sides feebly negotiated the wide gaps between them, the Japanese fleet continued heading toward Hawaii while operating under radio silence. This was critical because unbeknownst to the Japanese, the Allies' codebreakers were able to decrypt their communications long before Pearl Harbor. And though Japan was unaware that they had successfully broken the Japanese encryptions on their diplomatic communications, they assumed the U.S. would be monitoring their naval communications in the Pacific and thus had their radio operators sending out fake radio communications, fooling American eavesdroppers into believing their navy was still in the North Pacific near Japan itself.

As fate would have it, the USS *Enterprise* arrived at Wake Island on December 4th, 1941, just four days before Pearl Harbor (local time, since Wake lies beyond the International Date Line). The ship brought the F4F-3 Wildcats and personnel of Marine Fighting Squadron 211. In fact, the *Enterprise*'s delivery of the squadron to Wake accidentally ensured its absence from Pearl Harbor during the Japanese attack on December 7th.

The *Enterprise*

Major Putnam, head of Squadron 211, immediately toured the airstrip and presented Commander Cunningham with a verbal list of necessary structures – a secondary airstrip, hangars and revetments, and further leveling and clearing of the ground surrounding the existing landing strip. Putnam wrote a prophetic letter to his superior, in which he described himself as feeling like a "fatted calf" ready for slaughter in his new assignment. Neither he nor the other Americans on the island knew on December 4th of the imminence of Japanese attack. On the same day as Squadron 211, Assistant Superintendent Harry Olson flew to Honolulu on a Boeing 314 Clipper flying boat for some vacation time. His son, Ted Olson, remained behind on Wake.

Major Putnam's men painted their F4F-3s the regulation blue and gray upon their arrival. The Major also started dawn and evening patrols to increase the island's security, sending out four aircraft at a time. His 12 Wildcats represented a secret surprise for any Japanese attacking force. They had in fact been sent to the island in such secrecy that the men had not been informed of their destination, instead being told they would carry out a brief exercise. Accordingly, they arrived with no equipment whatsoever except for their aircraft and the clothing they wore when they set out.

Devereux's Marines labored feverishly to build machine gun and artillery positions, anti-aircraft batteries, and other defensive works, mostly using picks and shovels to excavate the coral. Work continued at a brisk pace up until the Japanese attacked.

The federal government still had a chance to connect dots on December 6, the day before the Japanese attacks were launched. At noon on that day, the Army intercepted and translated a message sent from Tokyo to Ambassador Nomura instructing him to receive an impending 14 part message that was to be considered a counterproposal to American negotiations, and he was instructed to deliver the message to Secretary of State Hull at 1:00 p.m. EST on December 7. That timing was meant to allow the Japanese to launch the surprise attack before the Americans received the message, but there was another clue that the Japanese were preparing for war. The communication also instructed the Japanese embassy to destroy its cryptographic equipment after receiving the 14 part message, meaning that they would no longer need to encrypt outgoing communications back. Such a step would only be taken if the Japanese had no intention of maintaining the embassy or using it for communications, which was a very clear sign that they were ready for war.

Almost simultaneously, as Roosevelt was sending a personal plea to the Emperor Hirohito, the Navy station on Bainbridge Island intercepted and began transmitting the first 13 parts of the message Tokyo was sending its ambassador in Washington. The message thus reached American officials in Washington around 3:00 p.m., and the Navy's cryptologists began translating it. Bainbridge Island intercepted the very last part of the message around midnight PST and sent it to Washington, where Army cryptologists decoded it and began sharing the communication. The 14 part message was not a formal declaration of war, but it made clear that negotiations were finished, and as a result warnings were sent out to American bases to have their guard up overseas.

Unfortunately, Admiral Harold Stark, Chief of Naval Operations, believed that previous warnings had been sufficient for Pacific installations, including Pearl Harbor, to be at a proper alert level, so he didn't bother waking up Admiral Husband Kimmel in Hawaii given that it was the dead of night. Meanwhile, early in the morning of December 7 in Washington, Army Chief of Staff General George Marshall ordered the dispatch of a potential warning of war: "Japanese are presenting at one p.m. Eastern Standard Time today what amounts to an ultimatum also they are under orders to destroy their code machine immediately Stop Just what significance the hour set may have we do not know but be on alert accordingly Stop." However, Marshall would be out on his Sunday routine and was unavailable for contact until noon, and the Army was suffering technical problems that prevented his warning from reaching Hawaii in time.

Marshall

Stark

As a result, those who had decoded and seen the Japanese communications would not be surprised when they heard about an attack on December 7, 1941. They would, however, be astonished when they heard where the attacks took place.

Chapter 2: War Comes to Wake Island

The sunrise above the western Pacific that morning was spectacular. The great orb slipped above the eastern horizon burning bright red, with its shafts of light spanning outwards and glinting off the polished wings of an airborne armada. As the sun was rising, nearly 200 Japanese aircraft were across the vast expanse of ocean. These were the elite aircrew of the Imperial Japanese Navy. Nothing if not romantic and spiritual, the young men from the land of the rising sun glanced out of their canopies and considered it a good omen.

At dawn that day, the air of Roi airfield in the Marshall Islands filled with the deep throbbing of bomber engines and the whir of spinning propellers. The sharp stink of aviation fuel mixed with the steady trade winds as the Emperor's soldiers prepared to deliver one of the day's surprise attacks against the Allies. As the sunrise glowed in the sky, the first of 36 Mitsubishi G3M "Rikko" Type 96 twin-engined bombers lumbered into the air above the tiny scrap of land and the gigantic expanse of the Pacific. Led by Lieutenant Commander Matsuda Hideo, the bombers fell into formation and pointed their noses towards Wake, 720 miles distant.

A G3M

Around the same time on Wake Island, the Marine bugler Alvin Waronker sounded reveille and the men left their barracks for another day of work after an interval of rest on Sunday. Major Putnam's dawn patrol of four Wildcats lifted off, buzzing over the low treetops of Wake to fan out over the sea, with Putnam himself piloting one of the aircraft. The men ate a quick breakfast of eggs, sausage, and hotcakes, then retrieved their tools for another day's toil on a sunny day in the 80s. Work crews climbed into trucks for transport to their assigned areas.

Shortly before 7 AM, the arrival of a pair of plain language Morse code transmissions from Hawaii shattered the day's developing routine: "SOS, SOS, Japs attacking Oahu. This is the real thing. No mistake. [...] Pearl Harbor under attack from Japanese planes. This is no drill! Repeat – this is no drill." (Moran, 2011, 22).

Due to the jury-rigged communications on the island, the radio operators could not transmit the information directly to Devereux by telephone or radio. Instead, they telephoned the staff sergeant in the K-18 transmitter trailer nearby. The sergeant scrawled the message hastily on paper, and gave this to a motorcycle courier outside. The Marine cyclist sped to Camp 1, where he gave the paper to the duty officer, Captain Henry Wilson, who rushed it into Devereux's tent after glancing at the contents.

Devereux, engaged in shaving, immediately tried to call Cunningham at Camp 2, but the commander had not yet reached his office and no other telephone link existed. The Marine leader therefore called on the services of Field Music Waronker again to use his bugle in sounding "General Quarters." Unfortunately, Waronker proved utterly incompetent at his task, blowing a series of incorrect calls so poorly that many of them proved barely identifiable.

After a brief time, Waronker accidentally sounded "General Quarters," then, identifying it as correct, blew it repeatedly. The Marines, who had listened with mocking disbelief to the preceding cacophony, downed tools and hurried to retrieve their weapons. However, Wake's defenders had no way to communicate with the Wildcats sent out on dawn patrol, while the rest of the aircraft could not be dispersed on the ground due to lack of revetments or even secondary airstrips.

As the Marines gathered, Waronker again shifted the bugle call to "Fire Call," causing some men to abandon their rifles and fetch water buckets. Eventually, sergeants running or driving between the positions with Devereux's orders corrected the chaos prompted by Waronker's calls.

Trucks drove along Wake's limbs, bringing ammunition supplies to each position from the central storage area – too small to be properly called an "ammunition dump." While some of the men stood on guard, and one gun in each 3-inch anti-aircraft battery remained manned, the other soldiers in each unit began digging foxholes and slit trenches while keeping their firearms ready to hand.

The island's leaders, both civilian overseers and military officers, agreed that the civilian workers would continue with their jobs until such time as action appeared imminent. Construction work therefore continued, and some men even carried on the task of neatly whitewashing the buildings for a planned inspection now likely to never occur.

The dawn patrol returned at 9 AM, and after hearing about the attack on Pearl Harbor, Major Putnam ordered another quartet of planes into the air. The patrol of four Wildcats, one piloted by Captain Henry "Hammering Hank" Elrod, first scoured the area south of Wake, then worked around toward the north. Vast cumulus towers, many of them producing rain squalls, now dotted the ocean, cutting visibility and forcing the Wildcats up to 12,000 feet.

Elrod

Elrod and his fellow pilots moved away to the north shortly before Matsuda Hideo and his 36 G3M "Rikko" bombers approached Wake from the south. Though flying at 10,000 feet on the approach, the experienced Matsuda noted a rain squall sliding onto the southern edge of Wake Island ahead. Forming into three V-shaped echelons of 12 aircraft each at Matsuda's command, the Japanese dropped to 2,000 feet and swept in on their quarry, hidden amid the squall's buffeting winds and rain.

The first group of bombers exploded out of the rain curtain almost overhead from the defenders' perspective. Instantly, the Japanese began strafing the Americans with incendiary rounds fired from 20mm cannons. Bombs dropped from the undersides of the craft, which one civilian witness initially interpreted as their wheels falling off. In response, the 3-inch anti-aircraft guns that remained manned while the work details prepared last-minute shelters quickly opened fire. Numerous .50 caliber machine guns, located in sandbag reinforced pits along the boomerang-shaped length of Wake, also opened fire, spilling streams of half-inch diameter bullets into the sky.

The Japanese planes ignored the incoming fire and strewed their bombs over the airfield with lethal accuracy. Densely saturated with 100-lb bombs, the airfield proved a death trap for the Wildcats still on the ground despite the attempt at dispersal. Direct hits smashed seven of the eight F4F-3s into scattered, burning debris, while the eighth suffered heavy but not catastrophic damage. Moreover, the airfield bombing inflicted immense casualties on Major Putnam's men, including Putnam himself, wounded by bomb fragments. Three pilots and 23 ground crew died, either blown to fragments in the bombing or dying from their wounds within a few hours. 3 more pilots and 8 additional ground crew suffered wounds, bringing the total number of Squadron 211 losses to 60% of its personnel put out of action immediately. 10 PanAm employees and 25 civilian contractors also died, with extensive damage to both camps and other facilities and equipment on the island.

The shattering Japanese attack lasted just 12 minutes, from 11:58 AM to 12:10 PM. During it, Sergeant Alton J. Bertels acted with a coolness and determination that drew the notice of Woodrow Kessler, later a USMC Brigadier General, though he noted that Bertels died of starvation and tuberculosis in a Japanese concentration camp a few weeks before the end of the war: "[W]hen the first bombs fell on 8 December, he became a gung-ho Marine. He was everywhere lending a hand in the defense. Danger gave him an added spark. [...] I have a distinct vision of Sergeant Bertels driving a bulldozer which he had found [...] as he came driving it up to the battery position, enemy planes appeared overhead. He drove with such concentration that it appeared he might not be aware of the danger [...] Some of the men caught his attention by waving and pointing to the sky. He [...] kept on driving until the bombs and straffing [*sic*] were actually falling around him. Only then did he jump from the dozer into a hole." (Kessler, 1988, 43).

During the raid, a Japanese bomb struck the 25,000 gallon aviation fuel storage tank near the airstrip, causing it to erupt into a catastrophic fountain of fire. The sea of burning fuel spread, setting off dozens of 55-gallon drums filled with aviation gas and turning part of the runway into a raging inferno. Some of the pilots died running for their Wildcats, machine-gunned by the Japanese gunners as they tried to get airborne and counterattack.

Unfortunately, the Japanese aircraft flew too low at around 1,500 feet for the 3-inch guns to engage them effectively, but too high for the .50 caliber machine guns. Some Marines fired their rifles at the twin-engined bombers, but none of the Japanese aircraft fell, however. The Japanese felt highly pleased themselves, as one of them, Norio Tsuji, recalled: "The pilots in every one of the planes were grinning widely. Everyone waggled his wings to signify 'BANZAI!'" (Heinl, 1947, 15).

The four-aircraft patrol returned from the north just in time to be greeted by the sight of thick black smoke gushing up from Wake's installations, and Japanese bombers vanishing southward into cloud cover. The four pilots briefly gave chase but the Japanese, with a head start, melted away like ghosts. When the pilots landed, "Hammering Hank" Elrod's propeller struck debris on the runway, putting his aircraft out of action and thus reducing the available Wildcats to just three.

Devereux, commanding the island, expressed his frustration that the radar unit promised to Wake Island's defenders had not yet arrived. Had this equipment been present, all 12 Wildcats would have met the Japanese in the air and quite possibly destroyed many of the slow, obsolete G3M Rikko bombers. Nevertheless, despite the catastrophic damage inflicted, the Marines still had fight in them. Prudently, they had scattered a considerable quantity of aviation fuel in six camouflaged caches amid the thick trees and undergrowth of Wake's interior, and these stashes, invisible from the air, remained completely intact.

Though all the aviation mechanics lay dead – alongside the dozens of other corpses placed in refrigerated storage – and the Japanese had destroyed all maintenance and repair equipment, Second Lieutenant John Kinney and Technical Sergeant William Hamilton volunteered to keep the aircraft running. Major Putnam colorfully promised them "a medal as big as a pie" (Moran, 2011, 39) if the pair succeeded at this new, unexpected task. Using parts scavenged from the wreckage and a few tools found among the civilian contractors' supplies, the two men performed practical miracles in keeping the last few Wildcats functional. Putnam also sent the last three Wildcats aloft again after refueling to protect them if another bombing raid occurred. Moreover, a PanAmerican Boeing Clipper in the lagoon, recalled from a trip westward to the Philippines due to the Pearl Harbor attack, suffered damage from machine gun fire but remained airworthy. The pilot, Captain John Hamilton, dumped a quantity of fuel and had the mail unloaded, enabling him to squeeze 25 civilian contractors aboard for a flight to Midway Island, still relatively out of harm's way.

After the raid, many of the men, who did not believe the Japanese could muster such an attack, maintained stubbornly that they had seen Nazi swastikas on the underside of the bombers' wings. They had, of course, actually seen the solid red "meatball" of Japan, but some of the Marines would remain unconvinced until Japanese troops actually landed on Wake Island. Regardless, during the rest of the day, the men, both military and civilian, worked tirelessly to build new defenses, including foxholes and trenches, in expectation of the next attack. Since most of Wake's telephone lines lay above ground, the bombing had severed many of them, necessitating repairs in most sectors. Dan Teters' 300 civilian volunteers now began their work in earnest, hiding caches all over the three islands so that no one bomb or series of bomb could destroy the garrison's supply of water, food, or ammunition.

As that took place, Kinney and his ad hoc crew, now increased by a few civilian and Navy mechanics, spent the day working on the least-damaged of the knocked out Wildcats. In the meantime, sentinels atop the 200-foot water tower scanned the sea and sky for signs of Japanese approach, but nothing menacing appeared for the rest of the day.

Chapter 3: Subsequent Aerial Attacks

By the time General Quarters sounded the following morning at 5:30 AM, Kinney and his crew had finished repairing the damaged Wildcat, enabling Major Putnam to send four F4F-3s aloft for the dawn patrol. In less positive news, some of the civilians had decamped to the brush overnight, taking supplies of food and water with them. These men remained in hiding until the surrender. Most of the civilians, however, showed themselves willing and eager to help in strengthening the island's defenses. Devereux picked out a group of civilians who had shown interest and aptitude in the Marines' weapons and placed them as a crew for a 3-inch gun which had remained unmanned up to that point. He assigned one veteran Marine to the gun to oversee the inexperienced civilian crew.

The Marines also "mined" the airstrip with buried dynamite charges, with wires leading to three separate emplacements in the area. These arrangements would enable them to destroy Japanese troop transports if the Japanese attempted to land them on the island airstrip. Devereux also created a "mobile reserve" of 12 men with four machine guns, with a truck for transport, under the command of Second Lieutenant Arthur Poindexter. These men could rush to any point where Japanese troops appeared to bring heavy firepower to bear against them, regardless of whether they arrived by sea or air.

The day began with labor under a clear, sunny sky. As with the day before, the Marines manned one gun in each battery while the rest worked. Dan Teters' civilians proved especially helpful with their bulldozers, rapidly constructing bomb-proof shelters at key points, though a later film about Wake wrongly depicted Teters as a useless obstructionist.

At 11:45 AM, 27 Japanese bombers under Lieutenant Commander Matsuda again appeared from the south, having flown at dawn from their Marshall Islands runways. With no clouds in the sky to hide them, the Japanese approached at 8,000 feet, high enough for the 3-inch anti-aircraft guns to fire at them effectively. Two Wildcats engaged the massed formation, and, despite torrents of Japanese fire, managed to shoot down a bomber at the end of one of the V groups, sending it plunging into the sea in a column of flame and smoke.

During the attack, the Japanese bombs hit a gasoline truck, triggering a huge detonation that obliterated the three men in its cab. They also damaged several 3-inch guns and one of the 5-inch naval guns in the Peacock Point battery. The heaviest strike, however, gutted the hospital at Camp 2, killing four Marines and 55 civilians. The hospital's two doctors worked frantically to drag the wounded out of the flaming ruins, ensuring a few survived.

Though this Japanese strike inflicted heavy damage, the Americans struck back fiercely. As the Imperial bombers wheeled away south, five left thick trails of black smoke behind them across the clean blue tropical sky. Before the aircraft flew out of visual range, one of them suddenly exploded, strewing its burning wreckage over the ocean surface. The rest limped back to base.

In the wake of this attack, Devereux studied the damage and came to the conclusion the Japanese used a systematic plan for bombing. He observed that they seemed particularly keen to knock out the 3-inch guns of Battery E, and one of the Japanese aircraft had circled the battery, clearly taking aerial reconnaissance photos for a subsequent attack. Working throughout the afternoon and night on Devereux's orders, the Marines moved Battery E to a new location, placing dummy guns in its place for the expected raid everyone figured would take place the next day.

With the hospital bombed, establishing new aid stations also received priority effort. The Marines quickly adapted two of the bomb-proof shelters to this role, setting up steel blast doors to keep the doctors and patients safe and placing generators for 24-hour electricity. Each facility had 21 beds and operated under the supervision of one of Wake's two doctors, Gustave Kahn (Navy reserve) and Lawton Shank (civilian).

Shooting down two Japanese planes and damaging at least four others improved morale greatly among the Marines. Though they expected a fresh attack the following day, Devereux overheard them joking and mocking the Japanese, in high spirits even despite their exhaustion.

High morale proved necessary as a third strike of Japanese bombers arrived punctually on December 10th. Nine of the bombers attacked the original position of Battery E, now occupied only by fake guns made of timber. Devereux's premonition proved accurate as the bombers, attacking from 18,000 feet, obliterated the "battery," smashing the fake guns to splinters.

However, while Devereux's prudence saved the battery, neither he nor anyone else on Wake could prevent the Japanese from striking their other targets. The bombers bombed Wilkes Island for the first time, heavily damaging two of the 5-inch naval guns there and destroying a 3-inch anti-aircraft gun. A bomb also struck a 125 ton cache of dynamite, unleashing a blast strong enough to strip most of the vegetation off the island and destroy a searchlight truck 2,500 feet away. Somehow, that blast only killed one Marine.

The bombers also attacked Peacock Point battery, but here their accuracy finally failed them. The bombs inflicted only trivial damage despite nine G3Ms targeting this single location.

As the Japanese assailed the island for a third time, the four remaining F4F-3 Wildcats rose to attack their massed formations. Flying with his customary aggression, Captain Henry Elrod swerved onto the tail of G3M Rikko, known to the Americans as a "Nell," and riddled the craft with machine gun fire. As the craft reeled downwards to the ocean burning, Elrod jinked his aircraft dexterously through the return fire of the Japanese machine gunners to engage and destroy a second G3M. Watching Elrod's skillful attack from the island, a Marine shouted enthusiastically, "Hammering Hank is sure giving 'em hell!" (Devereux, 1947, 64). That praise gave Elrod a nickname that entered history.

Chapter 4: The First Japanese Landing Attempt

While the bombers left with two less of their number after the December 10th attack and a third damaged and smoking from an anti-aircraft hit from a 3-inch gun, the Japanese pilots reported they had completely wiped out Wake's defenses. Officers noted that pilots of all nations in World War II tended to exaggerate the damage they inflicted on ground or ship targets, and the Japanese airmen proved just as susceptible. The explosion of the dynamite dump, which actually failed to damage the remaining defenses significantly, apparently convinced them of crippling harm inflicted on the Americans. Some of the Marines had underestimated the Japanese initially, and their opponents seemed quite willing to return the favor.

The commander of the Japanese invasion task force lurking beyond the horizon south of Wake, Rear Admiral Kajioka Sadamichi, wholeheartedly believed these rosy declarations. Showing the usual Japanese preference for night attacks, Kajioka's invasion flotilla moved into position in the darkness of a stormy night for an invasion to take place on December 11.

Kajioka

As it turned out, however, the Japanese attempts at stealth did little good. Sharp-eyed American sentries spotted objects moving out on the ocean surface at 3 AM on the 11th, as did the American submarines *Triton* and *Tambor*. One man on Wake's shore even believed he saw a light blink dimly in the darkness. The Marines quickly awakened Devereux, who walked down to the shore with several officers. Using "night glasses" – bulky binoculars designed for light amplification – the Marine officers quickly spotted a number of ships on the horizon.

The *Triton*

While the Marines prepared for battle in the predawn darkness, the Japanese experienced considerable difficulty loading their *Daihatsu*-class landing craft in the high seas. The landing craft bucked this way and that, flinging men off into the black, roaring ocean. Some of the 47-foot craft capsized and sank on the spot. Through it all, Kajioka's force of three light cruisers (the newest serving as his flagship), six destroyers, four transports (two of them hybrid destroyers), and two submarines persevered, and his adjutant later summarized some of the tactical planning: "[T]he plan was to have 150 men land on Wilkes Island and the balance, 300 men, on the south side of Wake Island to capture the airfield. The northeast coast was unsuitable for amphibious landings [...] We expected to have a rough time [...] we couldn't mass as many men as we considered necessary, and it was planned in an emergency to use the crews of the destroyers to storm the beach." (Heinl, 1947, 22).

While the transports struggled to deploy their landing craft and the luckless Japanese troops assigned to them, Kajioka's flagship light cruiser *Yubari* led the column of cruisers and destroyers inshore to launch a preparatory shore bombardment. The Japanese ships commenced firing at 5:22 AM, but the bombardment lacked the catastrophic thoroughness of American shore preparation later in the war, to the extent that Devereux thought the Japanese merely attempted to provoke return fire to pinpoint defenses. Eager to strike back, the battery commanders along Wake's southern shore persistently telephoned Devereux's headquarters for permission to open fire, but the Marine commander withheld permission and the island remained stoically silent during the first pass of Kajioka's ships.

Naturally, Corporal Brown, fielding calls from the battery commanders to Devereux's command post, received the full brunt of their rage. One of the commanders, whom Brown declined to identify later, shouted, "What is that little son-of-a-bitch doing? [...] Goddam it! We've been hitting targets at Pearl Harbor at 12,000 yards and the bastards are in to 7,000! What the hell is he waiting for? [...] Good Christ, they're at 6,500 yards! The bastards are practically on the beach! What in the hell are we up to!" (Urwin, 1997, 322).

Devereux's tactic worked, however. Failing to provoke even a single rifle shot or burst of machine gun fire, the Japanese column of ships turned and moved 2,500 yards closer inshore for a second bombardment run, now just 4,500 yards from Wake. Devereux's ploy had lured Kajioka into closing to an incautious range. At 6:15 AM sharp, Devereux gave the order to open fire, and his men, frustrated and desperate for action, immediately opened a heavy fire on the surprised Japanese ships. Peacock Point's Battery A engaged *Yubari*, with the battery commander, Lieutenant Clarence Barninger, standing on the roof of his command post hut the better to direct the fire.

Yubari

In the first morning light, the white fountains of the shell splashes straddled the *Yubari* abruptly. The Japanese gunners spotted the flash of Battery A's guns and returned fire immediately. One shell burst close enough to pepper the CP hut on which Barninger stood with shrapnel, but the lieutenant remained unscathed. For the rest of the engagement, the Japanese consistently fired short, coming nowhere near the battery again.

The *Yubari* immediately turned to flee also, zigzagging at high speed in an effort to avoid the American shells, but this effort proved vain, and Barninger described the results in a matter of fact manner: "The first salvo from our guns which hit her was fired at a range of 5,500–6,000 yards, bearing about 180 to 190. Both shells entered her port side about amidships just above the waterline. The ship immediately belched smoke and steam through the side and her speed diminished. At 7,000 yards two more hit her in about the same place [...] she turned to starboard again to try to hide in the smoke." (Moran, 2011, 57).

Though damaged heavily and listing visibly to port, the *Yubari* made good its escape. A Japanese destroyer raced between Battery A and the *Yubari*, laying a smokescreen in an effort to shield the retreating flagship, only for Barninger's gun crew to score a direct hit on the destroyer forecastle. The exploding shell persuaded the Japanese captain to order his own vessel to flee at top speed.

Meanwhile, Battery L on Wilkes Island outdid the success of Battery A on Peacock Point. Commanded by Lieutenant John McAlister, this battery lacked range-finding equipment due to a Japanese bomb hit the day before, but by observing the fall of shot and adjusting the guns' aim, McAlister walked his battery's fire onto the destroyer *Hayate* at a range of 4,500 yards. American 5-inch shells plowed into the Japanese destroyer, punching through its hull to explode amid the depth charges stacked densely inside. A terrific explosion followed, with the blast of orange fire and black smoke ripping the warship literally in half. Folding in on itself, the *Hayate* sank quickly into the sunlit morning ocean, taking all 176 men aboard with it and leaving no survivors. Any men who swam clear almost immediately fell prey to sharks.

The *Hayate*

For several moments, Battery L ceased fire as the gun crews noisily celebrated their unexpected triumph. However, one of their NCOs soon reminded them of their duty: "The gunners [...] stood cheering instead of shifting fire to the next destroyer. They were jolted [...] by a bellow from an old China Marine, Platoon Sergeant Henry Bedell: 'Knock it off, you bastards, and get back on the guns! What d'y' think this is, a ball game?' He was a thin, dried-looking man [...] but he had a voice that would have shamed a clap of thunder. [...] Somebody cracked, 'No wonder the Japs took off – they thought Bedell was yelling at them.'" (Devereux, 1947, 72).

The Japanese destroyers began moving at high speed, spreading smoke screens to cover the retreat of the other ships. McAlister's battery scored a hit on another destroyer, *Oite,* starting a major fire on board, but the vessel did not sink. The gunners also scored a solid hit on a transport, which fled into a dense smoke screen laid by several destroyers. In the process, the American gun crews fired so rapidly that Battery L exhausted its ammunition and eventually fell silent while the crewmen rushed to drag fresh boxes of shells to the guns. McAlister rounded up a band of civilian volunteers to carry more ammunition, but by that time, the Japanese had retreated far enough so that his men could only fire at extreme range.

At around 7:10 AM, several Japanese destroyers and destroyer-transports cleared the western end of Wilkes Island. This brought them into the field of fire of Battery B's 5-inch guns on Toki Point, Peale Island. Lieutenant Woodrow Kessler brought both of his guns into action immediately, firing at a destroyer tentatively identified as the *Yayoi.* The battery also engaged the destroyer-transports and the two remaining light cruisers of Kajioka's invasion force.

Firing at a range of 10,000 yards, the guns fired ten salvoes at the *Yayoi,* with a hit finally achieved and a fire started on board. With the first ship burning, Kessler ordered the guns to shift fire to the second vessel in the column, and just as the guns shifted fire, the recoil cylinder filling pipe plug blew out of Gun #2, disabling it through malfunction. The flying plug struck Corporal A.F. Terry in the side, bruising him massively and raising a gigantic 4-inch high contusion that bulged alarmingly through his uniform shirt. Kessler offered to send Terry to the aid station, but, after standing gasping for breath for a minute, the corporal refused all first aid and dragged himself to Gun #1, helping the men crewing it reload more quickly. Kessler shifted all of Gun #2's crew to #1, greatly increasing the rate of ammunition resupply.

In response, the Japanese opened fire on Battery B, using armor-piercing shells rather than high explosive, which, together with remarkable good fortune, saved Kessler and his men from serious harm. Kessler described the Japanese fire in his memoirs: "At first their shells burst with greenish-yellow picric acid blobs in the lagoon [...] Then they went over us to land on the north beach. Then they split the straddle and we were in the middle of their pattern [...] One shell was observed by the men at the gun to fly down the open path between the two parallel lines of ammunition passers to explode beyond without harming anyone." (Kessler, 1988, 51).

Despite heavy fire, only Kessler himself suffered an injury from Japanese action. A shelf fragment grazed the tip of his nose and drew an immense flow of blood. At first, his men believed he had suffered a serious head wound. However, once he wiped his face of its gory mask, one ordinary band-aid sufficed to patch the small cut. A shell also cut the battery telephone line, though the men soon repaired this.

After another 10 rounds, the Marines managed to hit the second destroyer as well. At this point, the second and third destroyers began laying smoke, and all remaining Japanese vessels turned abruptly away from Battery B's fire under cover of the smoke screen. Kessler spotted one of the transports, possibly the one hit by Battery L, and his gun crew shifted fire to it. However, at a range exceeding six miles and with their fire control equipment and sights damaged by the impact of their own firing, the Marines did not manage to hit the transport. That said, the ship did alter course to avoid their shells and retreat, at which point Major Devereux ordered the ceasefire.

Even as they moved out of range of the island defenses, with the weather now clear after a rainy night, the Japanese did not escape so easily against the American F4F-3 Wildcats still functional on Wake Island. Kajioka's ships had no air cover of their own, and like all IJN vessels, the training of their anti-aircraft gunners focused entirely on volume of fire rather than marksmanship (unlike American anti-aircraft crews), meaning a relatively small number of aircraft could sometimes attack and inflict considerable damage on large Japanese flotillas. Kajioka ordered his ships to make full speed back to Kwalajein, but the damage inflicted by the shore batteries slowed several of them, and they would not escape so easily. Major Putnam, along with Captains "Hammering Hank" Elrod, Frank Tharin (who lived until 1990 after surviving Japanese captivity), and Herbert Freuler, flew their Wildcats high above the action, watching vigilantly for Japanese air support.

Once no carrier aircraft appeared, Putnam and his squadron made a final sweep at 12,000 feet to ensure no Japanese aircraft approached Wake from an unexpected direction. Then they set off in pursuit of Kajioka's task force, with Putnam declaring over the radio, "Well, it looks as if there are no Nips in the air. Let's go down and join the party." (Urwin, 1997, 331). The clouds of the night had vanished, with a last filmy layer burning off in the sun, enabling the Wildcat pilots to easily spot the wakes of the ships many miles ahead on the deep blue ocean surface.

The American pilots swooped in to attack. Putnam attempted unsuccessfully to finish off the wounded *Yubari*, Kajioka's flagship. The Major streaked along the light cruiser's length, guns blazing as he attacked out of the morning sun. Ando Akira, a Japanese reporter aboard the flagship to record Kajioka's expected victory at Wake, witnessed and described Putnam's assault: "As soon as its low, roaring sound was heard in the wind like a murmur of the devil [...] a strafing and bombing from the enemy plane were poured into our ship while it wove through our machine-gun and high-angle gun fire. [...] A weird, metallic sound was heard, and the bridge was showered by enemy bullets." (Urwin, 1997, 332).

In the meantime, the other three Wildcat pilots targeted the obsolete light cruiser *Tenryu*. The men strafed the Japanese decks vigorously, destroying torpedoes and wounding five Japanese sailors, then dropped the small bombs carried by their F4F-3s. Each bore two of these 100-lb bombs in place of a pair 58-gallon drop tanks. The bombs mangled the decks and blew apart the torpedo battery.

The four Wildcats circled away, only returning to Wake long enough to refuel and rearm hastily before returning to the attack. The Marine pilots returned doggedly to the attack again and again until accumulating damage from anti-aircraft fire put two out of action. The other two, however, launched nine sorties apiece, hammering the Japanese relentlessly. Captain Koyama Tadashi later stated, "The American fighter pilots were admired for their skill and bravery," indicating that the Marines had risked death sufficiently to win recognition even from their enemies. Over the course of their attacks, the Marine pilots pumped 20,000 rounds of .50 caliber machine gun ammunition from their M2 Browning machine guns into the Japanese ships and dropped 20 of their 100-lb bombs in total.

After the first few missions, Thurin and Freuler switched out with the two mechanics, Kinney and Hamilton, who had managed to keep the Wildcats functional to this point with their remarkable skills at scavenging and jury-rigging. For his part, Hammerin' Hank Elrod tried to target the *Yubari* to supplement Putnam's attack, but instead misidentified the destroyer *Kisaragi* as his target. The two ships looked almost alike from the air, making the error easy, and Elrod struck the *Kisaragi* twice, hitting it with the full fury of his .50 caliber Brownings and dropping four 100-lb bombs on the vessel. One of these four bombs punched through the deck into the ship's innards before exploding, setting fire to the interior, where the Japanese stored large numbers of depth charges.

The *Kisaragi* halted for emergency repairs, then got underway again, leaving a long, plume-like oil slick on the sea behind it which made it even more visible to the relentless pilots. The destroyer crew received partial revenge, however. When Elrod made his attack run, the Japanese caught his aircraft with a burst of 7.7mm machine gun bullets, destroying the oil system. Elrod was forced to limp back to Wake Island, and the engine froze up just as Elrod reached the shores of Wake, forcing him to glide in and crash-land among the boulders on the beach. A group of men rushed forward anxiously, expecting him to be badly injured or dead, as Devereux recounted: "Putnam and I were among those who hurried down to pull what was left of Hammering Hank Elrod out of the wreck. He climbed out unhurt, but he wasn't thinking about the miracle of his escape. His plane was a total loss and he couldn't think of anything else. [...] He made only passing reference to the death blow he had dealt an enemy [destroyer]. What he wanted us to understand was, 'Honest, I'm sorry as hell about the plane.'" (Devereux, 1947, 75).

The *Kisaragi*

The wreckage of Elrod's plane

Out at sea, the other Marines continued their attacks on the Japanese. Kinney lined up his F4F for a run at the *Kisaragi* and had just begun his dive when the destroyer, still burning from Elrod's hit, blew apart in a thunderous column of fire, which spouted up to form a small mushroom cloud of black smoke and orange flame, while spray rose in a curtain around it. The fire had touched off the huge stock of depth charges aboard and blown the destroyer to pieces, again killing all 167 of its crew with no survivors. The ship sank 30 miles southwest of Wake Island.

The three remaining Wildcats, with Putnam, Hamilton, and Freuler at the controls, made another sortie and attacked the transport *Kongo Maru*. Freuler jinked expertly through the flak bursts and machine gun fire to land one of his 100-lb bombs in the transport's stern, starting a large fire, though with the numerous Japanese soldiers on board to supplement the firefighting crews, the Japanese soon managed to extinguish this blaze. A machine gunner also put two bullets through Freuler's engine, and the pilot barely made it back to Wake, albeit managing to land his plane intact.

Putnam and Hamilton flew one more mission at this point, strafing IJN Patrol Boat 33 and bombing the light cruiser *Tatsuta*, destroying its radio equipment entirely and collapsing most of its bridge superstructure. After this, Putnam deemed it too risky to launch another mission with only two Wildcats remaining, but the six Marine pilots and their four F4Fs had badly damaged Kajioka's already battered task force.

The Marines felt great elation and a sense of invincibility after forcing Kajioka's invasion force to flee southward with at least two ships lost. The Marines thought that they had sunk five ships, and a Japanese officer later told them, immediately after Wake's surrender, they had sunk nine. Both of these figures appear impossible. Regardless, the irrepressible if tone-deaf bugler Field Music Alvin Waronker drew an appreciative laugh from his officers when he declared loudly, "If we had a motor and a screw on this island we could pull over alongside of Japan and end this war in a hurry." (Urwin, 1997, 335).

Before anyone could bask in their excitement for too long, the Japanese interrupted the Marines' celebration with the arrival of 17 G3M bombers in two waves, somewhere between 9:15 and 10 AM (accounts vary). The Japanese pilots made an effort at surprise by approaching from the northeast, but the Americans spotted them and stood ready. Kinney and Second Lieutenant Carl Davidson flew on patrol in the last two Wildcats at the same time the Japanese raiders appeared.

Batteries D and E of the 3-inch anti-aircraft guns engaged the bombers as they swept over, distracting the Japanese to the extent they did not notice the Wildcats boring in at them at top speed. Highly excited, the two Marine pilots pushed in extremely close before letting loose volleys of .50 caliber machine gun bullets into the rear of the bombers. One bullet from a Japanese machine gunner punched through Kinney's canopy glass, smashed the left lens of his goggle, skimmed his temple, and burst out through the canopy rear. This represented the only damage sustained by the Americans.

On the other hand, the Japanese suffered some losses. Though they claimed the Americans only shot down two bombers, their records indicated 15 men KIA – exactly three bomber crews, and the number of bombers claimed by most of the Americans. Various people assigned the "kills" as one for each pilot and one for the flak batteries, or two for Kinney and one for the flak batteries.

After the bombers swept away – 11 more damaged, according to Japanese records – the Marine commanders allowed Battery E's crew to sleep. However, Devereux ordered Battery D on Peale to move at 2 PM. The Marines, assisted by some 200 civilian volunteers under Dan Teters, successfully moved the entire battery to a new position by the following morning.

A single F4F-3 Wildcat took off for dusk patrol with Second Lieutenant David Kliewer at the controls. Due to battle damage, the Wildcat took 15 minutes to start, and the other Marines also had doubts about Kliewer's utility in battle, due to the fact that he came from a family of religious pacifists, but the taciturn Marine offered no hint of his thoughts. On patrol at 4:30 PM, 25 miles southwest of Wake, Kliewer spotted a vessel on the surface far below him. As he dropped from 10,000 feet, the pilot identified the craft as a Japanese Type L4 submarine, lying fully exposed on the surface, probably charging its batteries and clearing hot, foul air out of the interior.

Kliewer quickly proved that the warrior spirit existed within him despite his pacifist upbringing. He immediately went into an attack dive, frantically unleashing streams of .50 caliber bullets at the long, low hull wallowing in the swell. The Marine pilot dived out of the sinking sun to preserve surprise, and managed to hit the craft with the heavy-caliber machine gun bullets.

Yanking his airplane out of its dive only at the last moment, Kliewer executed a right-hand 90-degree turn and attacked again. This time, Kliewer dropped his two 100-lb bombs. He launched them at so low an altitude that flying shrapnel from them punched holes through the wings of his Wildcat, and the explosions straddled the Japanese submarine, RO-66, at a distance of no more than 15 feet. Despite the fact the bombs did not hit directly, the shock of their explosions through the water pummeled RO-66's hull.

Kliewer returned to the attack again and again until he had expended all of his ammunition, then returned to Wake to report. Putnam took the second working Wildcat up and flew to the spot, hoping to catch the submarine still on the surface. Instead, he found an oil slick. RO-66, diving with a damaged and seriously weakened hull, struck another Japanese submarine below the surface – RO-65 or RO-67 – whereupon its hull crumpled entirely, sending the vessel and its whole crew to the bottom. The Marines had scored another victory.

Chapter 5: A Broken Promise of Relief

The Japanese response to their repulse over Wake bordered on denial and outright fabrication. Kajioka, who deployed his ships incompetently and then fled in a panic without giving fresh orders, went to great efforts to blame the weather for his failure, and Radio Tokyo broadcast announcements that the Japanese shot down American Wildcats over Wake at a rate of 7-12 daily.

Compounding the Japanese's problems, heavy rain squalls and a dense overcast came in overnight, completely foiling the efforts of a six-plane predawn raid on December 12th by massive Kawanishi H6K4 flying boats out of Majuro. The Wildcats sallied aloft but could not find the Kawanishis in the murk, just as the Japanese bombed the lagoon in the mistaken belief they attacked the airfield. However, Tharin managed to spot one of the H6K4s and followed it to clearer air away from the island, where he sent the flying boat into the sea with no survivors among its 9-man crew.

The usual midday bombing failed to arrive on December 12th, even as the Marines manned their guns in readiness for an attack. The Japanese air group stated that they made a bombing raid, indicating either falsification to maintain "face" or a failed raid that struck some open area of ocean rather than Wake. The Marines speculated that RO-66 provided a radio beacon for the raiders, though no record exists to confirm or deny this idea.

The Marines continued building defensive positions throughout the day, while the approximately 80 corpses in refrigerated storage received burial in a trench covered over with coral. Four Marines fired a salute over it, while Cunningham and Devereux attended along with a lay preacher.

The day's activities concluded with Kinney, who had worked with almost no sleep since the previous day's engagement, restoring a third Wildcat to working order by the time of the evening patrol. After this, Kinney finally lay down to sleep.

While the Marines fought and labored on Wake, trying to hold out, the US Navy organized tardy relief for the garrison, moving in an almost leisurely fashion. The American news services also inadvertently encouraged the Japanese by repeatedly broadcasting about how "small," "tiny," and "isolated" the Wake garrison was, an understandable if not misplaced effort to stress the heroism of the defenders.

Admiral Kimmel began preparing a relief force almost immediately after the Pearl Harbor attack, but one delay after another prevented these ships from sailing as quickly as needed. The *Tangier* carried a battalion of Marines to reinforce the island, and Task Force 12 would escort it. The USS *Lexington*, an aircraft carrier, formed the centerpiece of the relief armada. However, Task Force 12 could not sail until the USS *Saratoga* arrived from San Diego in order to transfer 14 obsolete but nevertheless welcome Brewster F2A-3 Buffalo fighters to the *Lexington* to augment Putnam's Squadron 221 with Marine Combat Squadron 211. Navy red tape demanded that the *Saratoga* have a destroyer escort to sail from California to Oahu, and the only destroyers available, three obsolete near-hulks, moved at a snail's pace. *Saratoga's* captain, complying with orders, dropped his ship's speed to a fraction of its actual rate of travel in order to keep its escorts in sight.

The USS *Lexington*

Kimmel

Moreover, Task Force 12 proved incapable of refueling at sea and had to return to Pearl Harbor to do so, wasting another day. Kimmel renamed the Task Force with the number 11 and decided to send it to the Marshall Islands, while forming a new Task Force, TF 14, around the USS *Saratoga* for the relief of Wake. This only introduced further delays.

President Roosevelt addressed the press about Wake Island on December 13th, once again inadvertently stressing the garrison's numerical weakness for any and all listening agents. He declared, "So far as we know, Wake Island is holding out, has done a perfectly magnificent job.

We are all very proud of that very small group of Marines who are holding the island. We have no further information today. They are holding out. We knew that very early this morning." (Moran, 2011, 61).

On December 14ᵗʰ, Task Force 11 finally left Pearl Harbor an hour before noon, commanded by the nervous Vice Admiral Wilson Brown. Due to delays in refueling *Saratoga*, the carrier and Task Force 14 only left Oahu on December 16ᵗʰ. Finally, Rear Admiral Frank Fletcher, spoiling for a fight and eager to relieve Wake, led his armada out into the blue vastness of the Pacific.

Roosevelt with Brown to his left

At this moment, military politics intervened fatally. Secretary of the Navy Frank Knox wanted a sacrificial victim to blame for Pearl Harbor, when in fact no sign of the impending attack had been apparent. Knox picked Kimmel, and forcefully demanded that Roosevelt see to his removal. The naval establishment agreed, and Kimmel received notice of his relief on December 16ᵗʰ, just as Task Force 14 sailed. Ironically, Knox's vindictive removal of Kimmel also removed the chance to gain an American victory before the end of the year, which Knox strongly desired to bolster American morale. If anything, Kimmel's removal ensured that a second shocking defeat, the fall of Wake Island, would hit the nation at the worst possible time, right around Christmas.

Knox

The reason why Kimmel's removal ensured the fall of Wake involved simple mathematics of time and space. Unlike the confident, aggressive Kimmel, his successor, Vice Admiral William Pye, proved extremely timid in the operational sense. He ordered Fletcher to refuel Task Force 14 constantly, presumably so it could "get away" if it met an overwhelming Japanese force. The only oiler with Task Force 14, *Neches,* moved at a soporific 12.75 knots in ideal conditions, while the 3 cruisers and 8 destroyers of the armada could sustain 36 knots and *Saratoga* could manage 39 knots. As a result, Pye's orders restricted the whole force to moving at just 12 knots to keep the *Neches* available for constant refueling. The ships therefore moved at a third of their typical cruising speed, inching over the ocean towards Wake.

Pye

Pye showed his nervousness by rescinding the orders given to Task Force 11 to attack Japanese island bases, literally minutes before Brown launched his carrier aircraft to do so. Instead, the Task Force would now proceed north to rendezvous with Task Force 14. Though all Brown's captains and most of his men wanted him to disregard the order and attack the Japanese islands – which might have altered Kajioka's second attack plan – Brown obeyed the command and turned north without firing a shot.

Ultimately, Task Force 14 came within 200 nautical miles of Wake during the crisis of the Japanese attack. At that moment, however, it received the order to halt and refuel once again, wasting the opportunity to intervene. Shortly thereafter, Pye ordered it to withdraw, completing the failure of the relief attempt.

Chapter 6: The Fall of Wake Island

Between December 12th and 22nd, the Japanese sporadically bombed the defenders of Wake Island, though often with little effect. The bombers operated at high altitude in most cases, affecting their aim. On December 13th, no Japanese raid occurred, but one of the Wildcats with Freuler at the controls crashed during takeoff, rendering it inoperable. The Japanese began bombing again the following day, attacking in the early morning with a few ineffectual Kawanishi flying boats and later with G3M bombers. Nonetheless, the bombers managed to hit one of the two still-serviceable Wildcats, setting it on fire. Lieutenant Kinney and two other men dashed into the flames and, through some combination of immense dexterity and luck, removed its engine intact without suffering injuries.

Not surprisingly, exhaustion took its toll on the men's wariness, including that of the commanders. The officers arranged for hot black coffee to be served to every post, battery, and station on the island regularly, especially at night, when vigilance represented a life-or-death necessity. The Japanese sometimes failed to bomb and at other times bombed the wreckage-strewn atoll relentlessly. Major Devereux noted other discomforts: "I remember the rats got worse. They overran us. [...] During one heavy bombing, a large rat was apparently driven berserk by shell-shock. It raced wildly around and around in circles and then dived into a foxhole, attacking the Marine crouched there. The crazed rat bit the man badly, fastening its teeth in his nose, hanging on while he beat it to death. The Marine did not think the incident as funny as his mates did." (Devereux, 1947, 92-93). During the time not spent in battle, the Marines entertained themselves by listening to – and insulting – the radio announcers in America who fulsomely praised them in extravagant terms. They also found some opportunity to laugh over the eccentricities of their fellow Marines.

Finally, on December 20th, a Consolidated PBY Catalina flying boat landed in the lagoon, crewed by two Navy pilots. The news brought by the men greatly cheered Cunningham, and, as the word spread, the rest of the island's inhabitants. The Navy men bore orders for Cunningham to prepare for the landing of reinforcements and the evacuation of most of the civilian contract workers, indicating a relief force close by.

The PBY left on the morning of December 21st carrying the Marines' letters to their girlfriends and families in addition to Devereux's report. But just a few hours later, a deeply ominous force put in an appearance in the sky over Wake Island when Japanese carrier aircraft swooped in for a raid, indicating that another invasion fleet lay close by.

Admiral Kajioka had indeed returned to make a second attempt on Wake Island. Once again, he deployed his ships with considerable incompetence, making them superb targets for Task Force 14 had Pye permitted Fletcher to attack. Four heavy cruisers sailed east of Wake, protected by no combat air patrol, and could have been easily destroyed by the USS *Saratoga's* aircraft. He also scattered the rest of his vessels, rendering them unable to offer each other mutual support. Kajioka received the four heavy cruisers as reinforcements, along with approximately 1,600 men of the Maizuru Second SNLF (Special Naval Landing Force), Japan's equivalent of Marines. Two minelayers and a seaplane tender joined the armada to serve as *ad hoc* transports. The Japanese also added the carriers *Hiryu* and *Soryu* to the force, giving Kajioka fighter and fighter-bomber support.

The December 21st raid by carrier aircraft struck at Battery D, finally hitting the determined anti-aircraft battery. One bomb killed Platoon Sergeant Johnalson "Big" Wright, clutching his lucky silver dollar as he usually did, by severing his left arm and driving it through his own body like a spear. His death sent the Marines at the battery into a killing rage, thanks to Wright's immense popularity among the other men.

Up in the sky, Freuler engaged the Japanese and managed to shoot down one aircraft, but with one Wildcat against dozens, he could do no more. A second raid arrived later in the day, this one composed of G3M bombers from Roi.

On December 22nd, the carrier aircraft struck again, and this time both Freuler and Davidson met them in Squadron 211's two remaining Wildcats. Six A6M2 Zero fighters escorted 33 Nakajima B5N "Kate" Type 97 dive bombers in their attack on Wake Island, and the two Marine pilots immediately attacked, dauntless in the face of even such odds. Cunningham gave the airmen full credit in his reports to Pearl Harbor: "Our escape from more serious damage may be attributed to the effectiveness of AA fire and the heroic actions of fighter pilots, who have never failed to push home attacks against heavy fire. [...] The performance of these pilots is deserving of all praise. They have attacked air and surface targets with equal abandon. [...] Their planes (two now remain) are full of bullet holes." (Sloan, 2003, 238).

Freuler shot down one Type 97, then engaged a second from the top rear. The Type 97 blew apart spectacularly in midair, damaging Freuler's aircraft but instantly killing all the men crewing it – including Petty Officer First Class Naburo Kanai, whose well-aimed bomb sank the USS *Arizona* at Pearl Harbor. Freuler's damaged plane came under attack by a Zero, and he faked a plunging dive to the sea to shake off the interest of his attacker. That same Zero pilot, Petty Officer Third Class Tahara Isao, subsequently turned on Davidson. Chasing one Zero and chased by Tahara in turn, Davidson flew out over the open ocean, where Tahara shot him down and killed him. The Kate dive bombers attacked all of the island's batteries, but failed to damage one gun or injure a single Marine. The Zeros had no better luck with strafing.

The last encounter put the two remaining Wildcats out of action permanently. Devereux sent Kinney to the aid station, nearly dead with exhaustion and a crippling case of diarrhea. The news that they no longer had any Wildcats depressed many of the Marines, who now felt helpless against Japanese air attacks. The few remaining airmen, including Hammering Hank Elrod, volunteered to serve as infantry.

The final night of the defense of Wake brought heavy darkness and rain squalls. One Marine, anonymous in the gloom, opined, "It's blacker than the inside of a cow." (Urwin, 1997, 443). The sound of wind mixed with the thunderous sound of open-ocean breakers slamming into the coral reef a few yards offshore. Masked by this profound darkness, Kajioka ordered his men to land on Wake at 2 AM.

Once again, incompetence still dogged the Japanese efforts. The two cruisers *Tatsuta* and *Tenryu* attempted to bombard Peale Island at 1 AM, but they merely fired at the ocean many miles to the north instead. The Marines observed the mighty flashes above the sea to the north, which alerted them to Japanese activity, and soon the whole island force stood to arms, peering into the darkness with their weapons at the ready. Many of the men later confessed to feeling a sensation of creeping dread at the sight of the inexplicable flashes.

At 2:30 AM, the Marines spotted the dark shapes of Patrol Boats 32 and 33 moving inshore in the south. The sound of landing craft motors at 2:53 prompted the Marines to switch on huge, 60-inch truck-mounted Sperry searchlights despite an earlier false alarm at Toki Point. Devereux, numbed by exhaustion, failed to order star shells fired, which might have provided enough illumination to turn back a landing before the shore.

The first wave of 900 Japanese SNLF troops moved inshore in a mix of landing craft and rubber boats. This required both skill and daring, since a powerful wind blew over the ocean, turning it into a wildly heaving and churning chaos of black water in almost pitch darkness. The sudden glare of the searchlight on Wilkes Island revealed the ocean just offshore thick with Japanese landing craft, and the Marines opened fire with .50 caliber machine guns from their Wilkes Island position. The Daihatsu landing craft's armored hull deflected most of the bullets, but some chopped through the skulls of Japanese soldiers incautious enough to look over the sides. The Japanese managed to shoot out the searchlight after it illuminated the beaches for about a minute, but the Marines kept firing.

The first Japanese rushed ashore near Clarence McKinstry's Battery F on Wilkes Island. The SNLF troops sent up a red flare to inform the rest of the Japanese that they had gotten a foothold on Wilkes, but the Japanese near Kuku Point fared less well. A second searchlight switched on in time to illuminate three boatloads of Japanese just offshore. Private First Class Erwin Pistole instantly opened fire with his .50 caliber machine gun, hosing down all three rubber boats and their occupants. Though the searchlight flicked off due to an electrical short, not one Japanese soldier from the three boats lived to reach the shore, either shot by Pistole, drowned, or pulped against the coral reef by massive waves.

As the Japanese charged forward, McKinstry and his men abandoned Battery F after disabling the guns. The SNLF troops halted there, busying themselves with erecting dozens of Japanese flags from every high point in sight. While it may have seemed like a waste of time, this exercise actually exerted a powerful influence over the battle's outcome. They also cut the American telephone wires on Wilkes Island.

Four groups of Marines now operated on the island, under McKinstry, Corporal Lillard Johnson with a .30 caliber machine gun section of 8 men on Kuku Point, the pugnacious Lieutenant McAlister, and Captain Wesley Platt, who inspired his men with a good-humored approach to leadership that won them over to following him readily into any danger. As the sun came up in the clearing sky, each group, though separated from the others, decided to set out and hunt down the Japanese. The groups began their individual sweeps of Wilkes Island, naturally converging on Battery F, killing all Japanese they met as they did so. One group of Japanese raised a shrill battle cry as McKinstry and his 24 men moved towards them, but the Marines –

mostly Southerners – drowned them out with the Rebel Yell. Moving forward in a battle fury, McKinstry and his men wiped out every SNLF soldier in the group they confronted.

As the Marines pressed the SNLF men back to their final position at Battery F, American losses in killed and wounded began to mount. The vicious close-range firefights resolved themselves with rifles, pistols, and bayonets as combat-frenzied men slipped from cover to cover, hunting each other through the dawn scrub of Wilkes Island.

Eventually, terror began to overwhelm the Japanese. They started huddling together in panicked clumps, trying to hide behind each other, which only enabled the Marines to cut them down with bursts of machine gun fire or hurled grenades. Captain Platt alone killed 12 Japanese trying to burrow under a bulldozer with several grenades.

The last 30 Japanese crowded to the abandoned searchlight truck and fought to crawl under it. The Americans approached this writhing heap of terror-stricken men cautiously, but the Japanese did not attempt to surrender. Instead, one shot Pfc. Severe Houde in the face, making his cranium explode. A second shot Pfc. "Gunny" Marshall in the gut, causing him to collapse in agony. Corporal Lillard Johnson, carrying his .30 caliber machine gun, responded by sitting down and throwing his weapon into position, his movements quick with rage. He released the traversing clamp and "kept the trigger on the machine gun depressed and watched the bullets going where I wanted them to go [...] Only every fourth bullet was a tracer, so I realized how severe the machine gun fire was as shrieks and screams came from the Japanese as their bodies winced and contorted and their arms and hands flayed in the air. Methodically from left to right I had attempted to spray bullets into every Japanese body visible." (Urwin, 1997, 472).

When Johnson expended his first 250-round ammunition belt, he loaded a second, loosed that into the Japanese, and kept pressing the trigger for several seconds before he realized that the stream of bullets had ended. A sweep of the bush yielded two wounded prisoners and 94 corpses. A few Japanese, shamming, leaped up and tried to bayonet Marines when they got close, but the Americans still operated on a hair trigger, their reflexes sharpened by adrenaline, and managed to shoot all of these individuals with no further losses.

With that, Captain Platt discovered that he and his "leathernecks" had completely wiped out the Wilkes Island attack force, and the men set about tearing down the Japanese flags festooning Battery F, but as soon as they did, Japanese carrier aircraft battered the island with bombing and strafing. With all their guns now out of action, the Marines could not respond to the Japanese other than with .50 caliber machine gun fire.

The Marines tried putting the Japanese flags back up, but carrier dive-bombers continued to pound Wilkes, forcing them into the brush despite their victory. By this time, it was almost two hours after noon. Dive-bombers also struck Peale Island, and Kessler noted a peculiarity of the attacks: "[T]eir bombing was not effective [...] although it was quite deafening. Apparently their bombs were fused with armor-piercing noses so that they did not explode horizontally on earth contact [...] Instead, the explosions were delayed until the bombs had penetrated the coral sand and rock to a depth of over twelve feet. The explosions were in the nature of a fountain." (Kessler, 1988, 69).

Meanwhile, Second Lieutenant Robert Hanna headed the defense of the main island. When the two Japanese patrol boats (nearly destroyer-sized vessels) beached themselves on the southern shore of Wake, Hanna took over Battery H and fired some 20 shells into Patrol Boat 32 until a shot hit the munitions aboard and set off a spectacular chain of blasts. Uchida Company of the SNLF leaped over the sides of Patrol Boat 32 and fought towards shore through the violent surf. The illumination provided by the burning vessel let the Marines mow down the Japanese by the score as they landed, though some managed to shelter behind coral outcroppings. The glare of fire also illuminated Patrol Boat 33, likewise beached farther along the shore, with the men of Itaya Company pouring over its sides. Battery E under Lieutenant William Lewis opened fire with its 3-inch guns, setting the shells to explode as airbursts over the beach, raking it with lethal fragments.

A destroyed Japanese patrol boat during the battle

Marine machine-gunners moved up to add to the firepower directed against their assailants, and soon the Japanese corpses stacked one atop another as the SNLF troops continued trying to push ashore. Japanese war correspondent Ibushi Kiyoshi, among the men debarked from Patrol Boat 33, noted, "Shells burst directly over our heads, and there was a continuous and intense horizontal fire from the high-angle guns...We hugged so close to the ground that our helmets dug into the earth." (Wukovits, 2003, 181). A friendly Japanese interpreter later advised the American crews that together, Batteries H and E had killed more than 330 Japanese troops, over a third of the total first landing wave, and that the SNLF soldiers sought revenge against those Marines in particular.

At this point, Devereux, commanding from a relatively remote location, made a fatal mistake. With essentially no evidence, the Marine major decided Battery E was contributing nothing to the fight and ordered Lewis to cease fire. Lewis obeyed, allowing the Japanese to surge inland into the thick brush. With approximately 300 Japanese about to overrun Hanna's battery, Devereux ordered Putnam to take his remaining pilots and ground crew as infantry to protect the position. Putnam set out with 12 men, including Hammering Hank Elrod, and 14 civilian contractors who refused to be turned away. They carried spare ammunition for the Marines.

Though the Japanese had the numerical advantage, they fought with the inexplicable, peculiar tactics they often showed throughout the war even when these seriously hampered them. The SNLF troops first fired flares, trying to illuminate the Americans, and then stood up and made banzai charges in clusters of six or eight men, running through their own illumination as they eschewed bullets in favor of bayonets. Conversely, the Americans relied on their firepower and marksmanship, cutting down large numbers of these brave but rather foolhardy assault troops. The Japanese, balked by the heavy fire, dragged a few captured civilians forward, removed their clothing, and tortured them by gradually mutilating their genitals with bayonets. The SNLF hoped that the agonized screaming and pleading of the men being slowly castrated would prompt the Marines to charge forward recklessly. Though the ghastly sounds infuriated the Marines, they held their position, waiting for targets.

Finally, a group of Japanese worked their way onto the airfield, from which the Marines could not dislodge them. As morning came, the Japanese finally overwhelmed the aviation Marines under Putnam, at heavy cost. John "Pete" Sorenson, one of the toughest civilian contractors, roared curses at the Japanese and pelted them with coral rocks until they shot and killed him. Hammerin' Hank Elrod temporarily routed most of the remaining men of Uchida Company, first wielding a Thompson submachine gun, then, after killing the gunner, retrieving a Japanese light machine gun and attacking with that, bellowing "Kill the sons of bitches!" as he charged and spraying anything that moved.

Miraculously, Elrod survived this attack, falling back to the battery pit with Hanna, Putnam, and the few remaining Marines and civilians. Two of the civilians, Paul Gay and Robert Bryan, assisted the Marines in fighting, the former firing a pistol and the latter lobbing grenades. The two men resolved to kill themselves rather than fall into Japanese hands and suffer the mutilation of their genitals inflicted on the other captured civilians. Ultimately, a carrier aircraft spared them that necessity by strafing the battery and riddling both men with bullets. Hammerin' Hank Elrod also fell dead, shot by an SNLF soldier as he rose to hurl a grenade.

Elsewhere on the main island, Arthur Poindexter and his mobile reserve prowled through the darkness, counterattacking any Japanese they encountered. At one point, Poindexter and his men found two Japanese landing craft trying to batter their way through the coral reef some distance from Peacock Point at the tip of Wake's "chevron." Poindexter and three men, despite fire from the Japanese, ran down onto the beach and successfully hurled hand grenades into both landing craft, killing or badly wounding all the men on board.

Poindexter, working largely on his own initiative, set up a defensive line across Wake near Camp 1, made up of 10 machine guns backed by a line of approximately 50 riflemen. The Japanese made a few weak attempts on this line but soon abandoned their efforts, so at 9 AM, Poindexter decided to advance and retake the airfield. Leading his men personally, Poindexter moved swiftly over the airfield and nearby terrain, catching the Japanese unprepared. SNLF squads ran in a panic into bomb craters, where the Marines killed them with grenades.

After clearing the airfield, Poindexter found himself confronted by larger, better organized Japanese forces. He halted his men temporarily while moving his machine guns into a position to break up the Japanese line. Poindexter meant to keep on with his attack. However, at that moment, Major Devereux appeared on the road, walking with a group of Japanese under a white flag. The Major had surrendered the island and now toured it with the Japanese, ordering his men to stand down.

Devereux had remained in his headquarters throughout the action, even after the Japanese cut most of his communication lines and thereby rendered the HQ useless. He had a force of 60 troops with him but apparently never even considered using them to counterattack the Japanese, instead ordering them to remain in position and defend the headquarters. In fact, Devereux assumed that every unit he lost contact with had been annihilated, never even bothering to step outside his command building to hear the continued firing from all over the island that proved the Marines remained active and even successful in many areas. The report of Japanese flags visible on Wilkes Island had led him to believe right away that the Marines there had suffered annihilation.

As a result, Devereux sent no patrols or runners to attempt to determine the situation anywhere on Wake. Instead, when approximately a dozen infiltrating Japanese began firing weakly at his 60 men, Devereux interpreted the occasional shots he heard as being attacked so heavily that his men would soon be overrun. He transmitted his bleak estimates to Cunningham – via the only telephone line still open – and effectively persuaded the island commander to surrender. Once Cunningham gave the order, Devereux immediately and vehemently placed all blame for the surrender on Cunningham.

The dispirited signals from Devereux and Cunningham prompted Admiral Pye to order the withdrawal of Fletcher's two Task Forces, poised to relieve Wake. Fletcher flew into a rage at the new orders, and his officers urged him to disobey the command and advance to Wake with his powerful unified force. Indeed, the Marines on the *Tangier* nearly mutinied at the news, but Fletcher obeyed. In a moment, Pye became the most hated man in the Navy; many men believed he had chosen to lose Wake Island, and Pye found himself relieved of command on December 31st. Though he retained his admiral's rank, Pye never held another command.

During the next 6 hours, Devereux moved across Wake under escort by SNLF troops with a white flag. At every turn, he discovered that the men he dismissed as wiped out were, for the most part, alive, active, and even locally successful. His appearance and order to surrender produced stunned disbelief among the men who had until then been holding out against, or even counterattacking and wiping out, Japanese assault forces.

Thanks to the unnecessarily hasty surrender, the Marines suffered just 28 killed in action during the final battle for Wake. The Japanese, by contrast, sustained more than 500 men killed, over half of the first wave. Official Japanese reports claimed only a few dozen killed or wounded, up to 150, but other evidence strongly contradicted these claims. Japanese doctors told the Americans they treated that at least 500 SNLF troops lay dead, while several Japanese reporters who came ashore the next day reported "mountains" of Japanese corpses on the beach and Wilkes Island, lying on coral sand stained red with blood.

Chapter 7: The Aftermath

The Marines had acquitted themselves with extreme skill, bravery, and professionalism during the defense of Wake, showing extraordinary resourcefulness, fighting prowess, and determination in the final stand on December 23rd. Arguably, they won the first engagement and could have thrown back the initial assault entirely had Devereux shown any initiative rather than surrendering with no information.

Unfortunately, this success only exacerbated their opponents' anger. The ordinary Japanese soldiers, enraged by their massive losses, stripped and tied their prisoners and gathered them in front of a line of machine guns. Thankfully, before they could massacre the Marines, Admiral Kajioka came ashore. Dressed in a spotless white uniform, Kajioka ordered the Marines treated like prisoners of war.

This ended the immediate threat of execution, but not the hardships endured by the American fighting men. Sent to prison camps in China, they endured starvation, brutal beatings, disease, and every kind of mistreatment. Some died and a few suffered summary execution at the whim of their sadistic captors.

When freed in 1945, the prisoners sometimes sought revenge. One group of Marines seized and lynched a Japanese overseer formerly keen on beating prisoners at every opportunity. Pfc. Jacob Sanders hunted for a guard who had slashed open his face with a cane, intending to kill him, only to discover the man had managed to flee: "I really scared myself thinking that I would want to kill someone, but his treatment was so brutal that I felt it was called for." (Wukovits, 2003, 245).

In other cases, the Japanese attempted to smooth over their mistreatment of the Americans by asking to shake hands and be friends, or by supplying large quantities of beer to the newly released prisoners. The latter, recalling the torments inflicted on them by the men now professing friendship, drank toasts to the "atom bomb," of which they had heard rumors from their guards.

After the campaign, the Japanese kept 98 civilian contractors on Wake as slave labor. After an air raid in 1943, island commander Sakaibara Shigematsu ordered the men massacred with machine gun fire. One man survived briefly, cutting the message '98 US PW 5-10-43' into a coral boulder, where it remains visible today. The Japanese soon recaptured the man and beheaded him.

The 98 Rock

The Japanese garrison of Wake surrendered on September 4th, 1945. The Americans subsequently hanged Sakaibara for ordering the massacre of civilian POWs. Out of 433 military prisoners taken, the Japanese executed 5, and 15 more died in captivity, with 413 eventually returning home. Out of 1,104 civilian POWs, the Japanese killed 98, 82 more died, and 924 – including the now 26-year-old Ted Olson – returned to the United States.

The men who survived Japanese captivity and returned underwent considerable culture shock upon their return to normal society. One Marine, Guy Kelnhofer of Manitowoc, Wisconsin, "stared in wonderment at a man mowing his lawn. 'The lawn cutting,' his wife later wrote of the incident, 'such an ordinary and peaceful activity, struck my husband as an utterly bizarre behavior.'" (Ells, 2001, 59).

Though Wake Island fell, the tough, ferocious resistance by the Marines immediately entered American legend. Even Devereux, whose command performance was understandably dubious amongst his men on the scene, became a towering figure of resistance, with the false quotation "send more Japs" put into his mouth. Arguments over the surrender aside, the Marines had indeed acquitted themselves superbly, from Putnam's fliers to the low-ranking officers whose personal initiative turned the Japanese landings into a costly bloodbath for the SNLF troops. The civilian contract workers helped with exceptional courage as well, greatly assisting the defense.

Though the immediate news of Wake's loss initially dampened American morale, the heroic defense eventually strengthened American resolve. As General Alexander Vandegrift declared during the celebration of Devereux's return, "Throughout the war the slogan of the Marine Corps always was remember Pearl Harbor and remember Wake." (Wukovits, 2003, 252).

Online Resources

Other World War II titles by Charles River Editors

Other titles about Wake Island on Amazon

Bibliography

Devereux, Peter. *The Story of Wake Island.* New York, 1947.

Ells, Mark David Van. *To Hear Only Thunder Again: America's World War II Veterans Come Home.* Lanham, 2001.

Gilbert, Bonita. *Building for War: The Epic Saga of the Civilian Contractors and Marines of Wake Island in World War II.* Haverstown, 2012.

Heinl, R.D., Jr. *The Defense of Wake.* Washington, D.C., 1947.

Kessler, Woodrow M. *To Wake Island and Beyond: Reminiscences.* Washington, D.C., 1988.

Moran, Jim. *Wake Island 1941: A Battle to Make the Gods Weep.* Botley, 2011.

Sloan, Bill. *Given Up For Dead: America's Heroic Stand at Wake Island.* New York, 2003.

Urwin, Gregory J.W. *Facing Fearful Odds: The Siege of Wake Island.* Lincoln, 1997.

Wukovits, John. *Pacific Alamo: The Battle for Wake Island.* New York, 2003.

Free Books by Charles River Editors

We have brand new titles available for free most days of the week. To see which of our titles are currently free, click on this link.

Discounted Books by Charles River Editors

We have titles at a discount price of just 99 cents everyday. To see which of our titles are currently 99 cents, click on this link.

CPSIA information can be obtained
at www.ICGtesting.com
Printed in the USA
LVOW04s2148150117
521025LV00015B/830/P

9 781537 259468